FIND CHAFFY

by Jamie Smart

BARRON'S

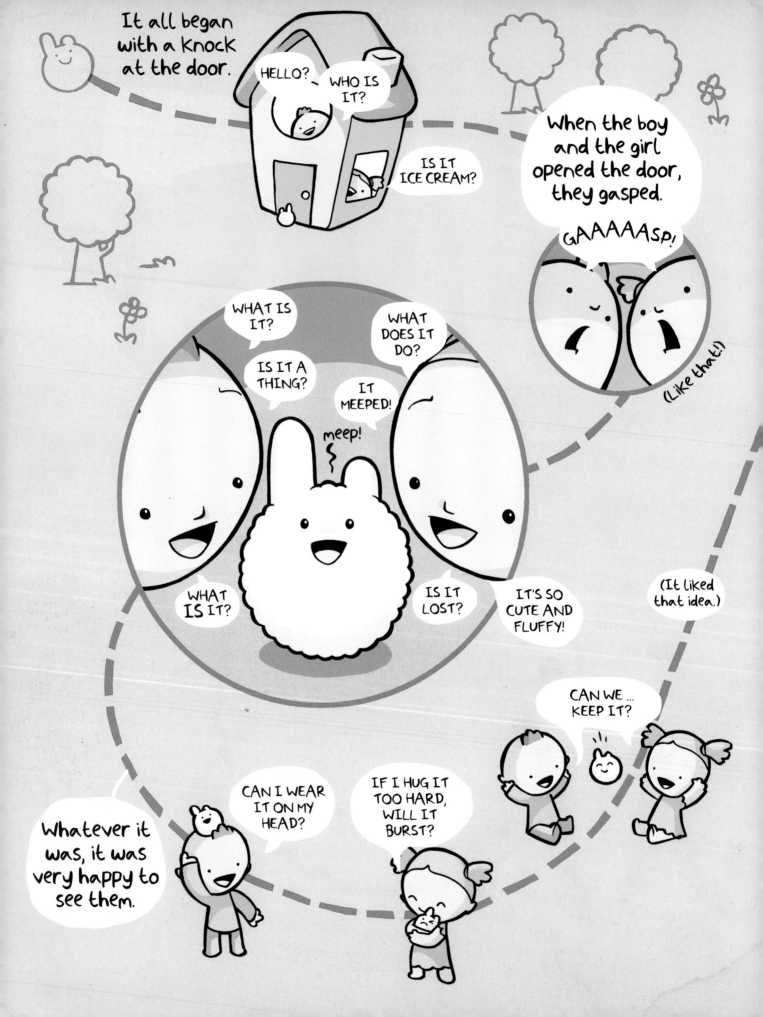

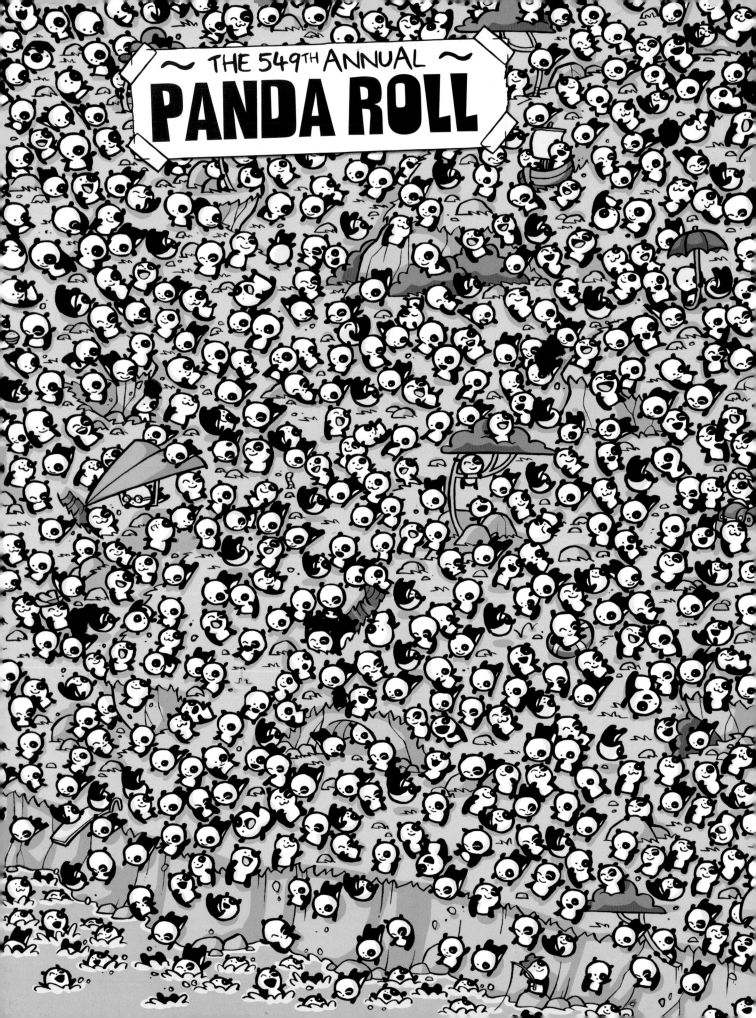

LOST

10 Chaffies
to find!
(But one looks a
little different...)

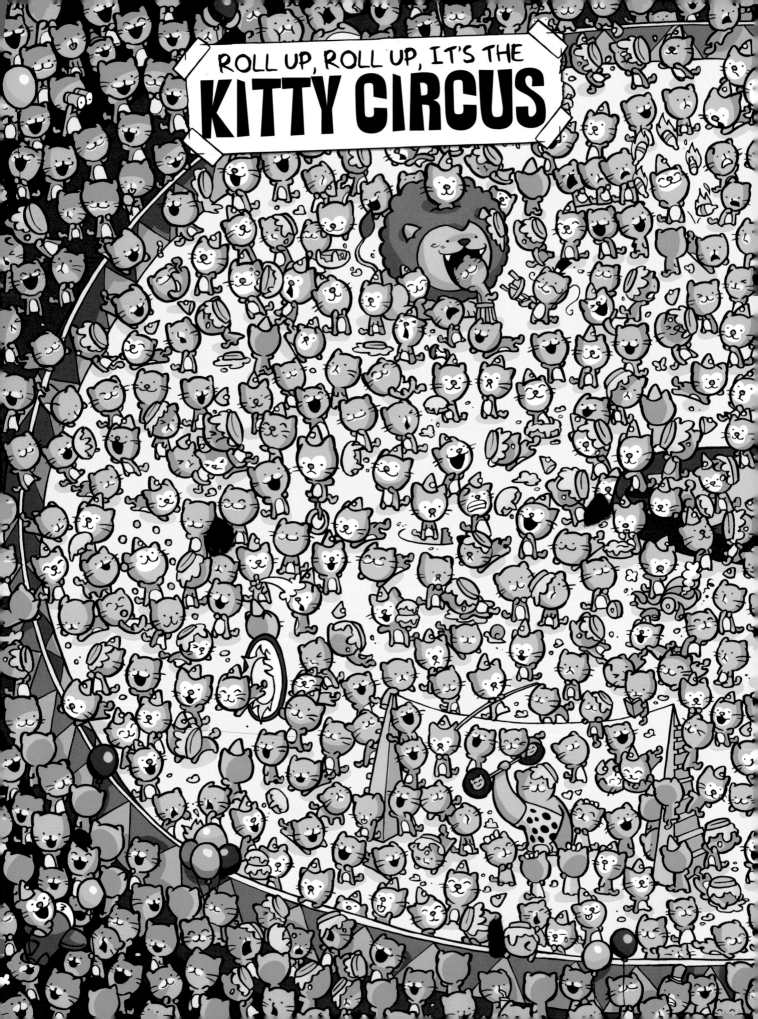

LOST

9 Chaffies to find!
(But one looks a little different...)

FLUFFY

LOST

8 Chaffies to find!
(But one looks a little different...)

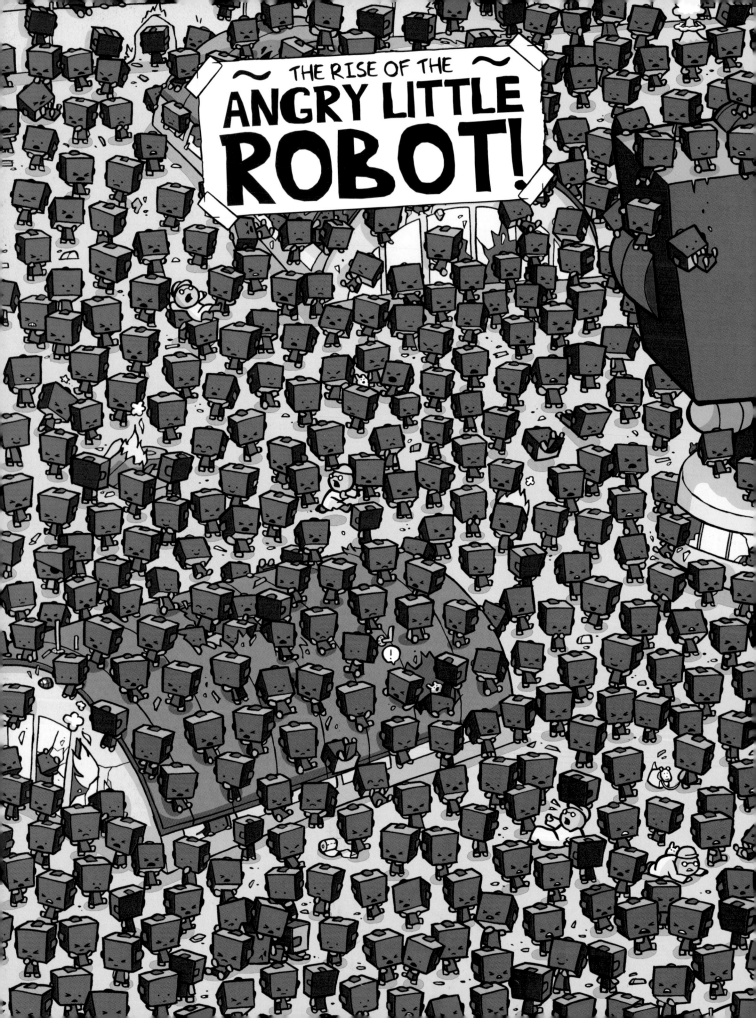

WELCOME!

LITTLE ROBOT
TECHNOLOGIES INC.

LOST

7 Chaffies to find!
(But one looks a little different...)

Did you find all 7 Chaffies?

1 2 3 4 5 6 ... 7?

BZZ!

Wait a minute, one of the Chaffies looked just like a ROBOT!

But can you TALK like a robot, Chaffy?

BZZ!

BZZ!

BZZ!!

Oh, you really CAN! And you've calmed all the robots down.

(Also, you make an EXCELLENT antenna for their T.V.)

So, Robot Chaffy stayed behind to help the robots clear up the silly mess they'd made, and the other Chaffies continued on their way...

#

LOST

6 Chaffies to find!
(But one looks a little different...)

THE END IS NIGH

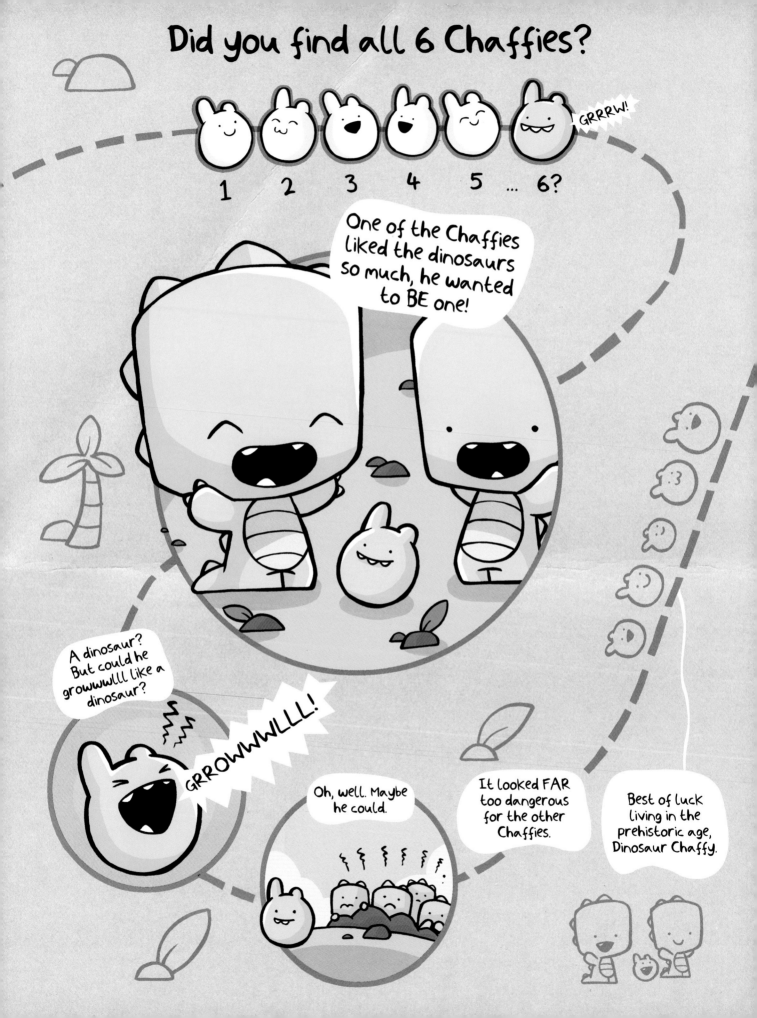

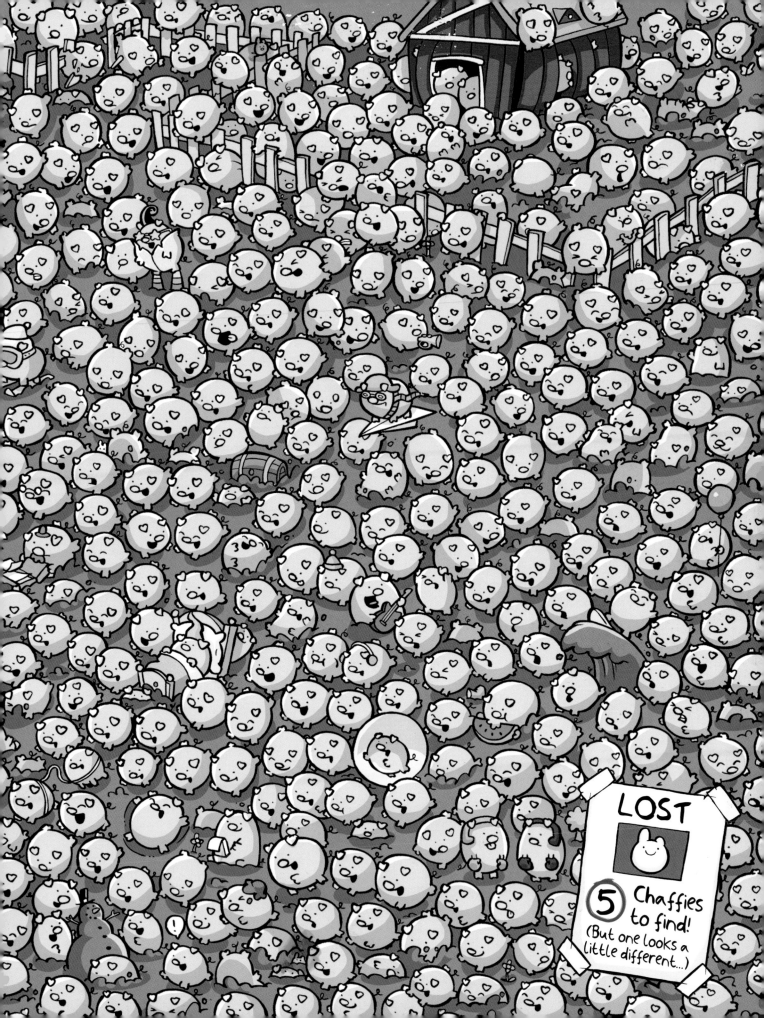

LOST

⑤ Chaffies
to find!
(But one looks a
little different...)

Did you find all 5 Chaffies?

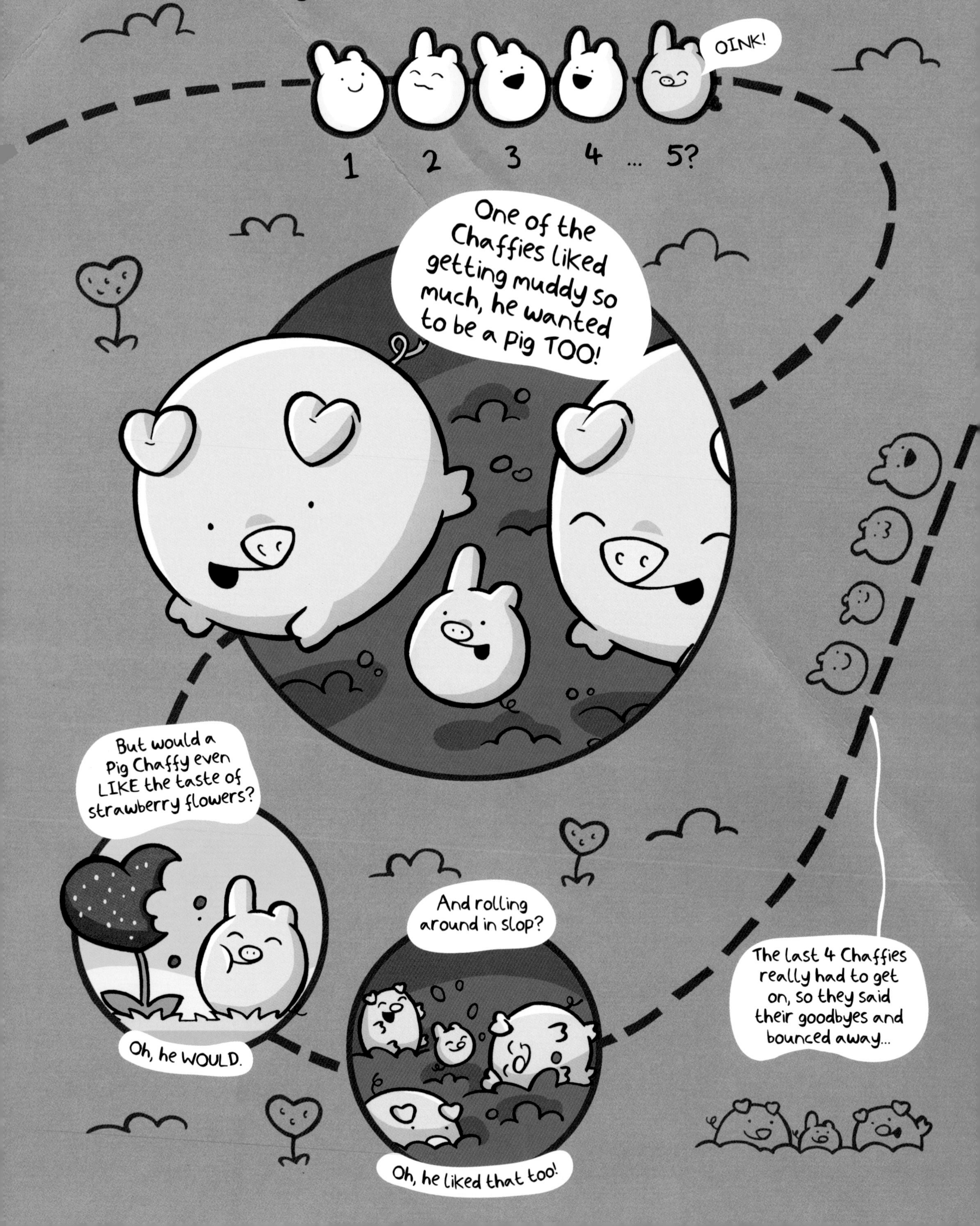

LOST

4 Chaffies to find!
(But one looks a little different...)

Built a rudimentary aircraft!

3,2,1 WOM

Tried on some clothes!

Lived in a cave! (For a bit...)

But, as they trekked up a steep mountain, a strange figure ran past!

A ... NINJA?
And another?
Another ninja?
And ANOTHER ninja?

And the Chaffies were right in the middle of it!

LOADS of ninjas, all competing in the Great Ninja Challenge. The first ninja to reach the rare green flower at the top of the mountain wins!

LOST

3 Chaffies to find!
(But one looks a little different...)

See-sawed!

Ate Spughetttty!

Went dancin'!

And found themselves on the edge of the woods.

Look! A picnic area! Maybe the humans there could help the Chaffies find their way home?

BEARS? Oh no, the smell of food has brought all the bears out of the woods!

All of a sudden, the humans began to run away!

LOST

② Chaffies to find!
(But one looks a little different...)

Did you find BOTH Chaffies?

GRRF!

1 ... 2?

Mmm! With all that delicious food lying about, one of the Chaffies decided that being a bear had its advantages.

One last Chaffy, all on his own. He must be nearly home by NOW!

But if Bear Chaffy stayed behind, there'd only be one Chaffy left!

?

Would he REALLY choose food over Chaffy?

Oh well.

chomp

chomp

Guess he would.

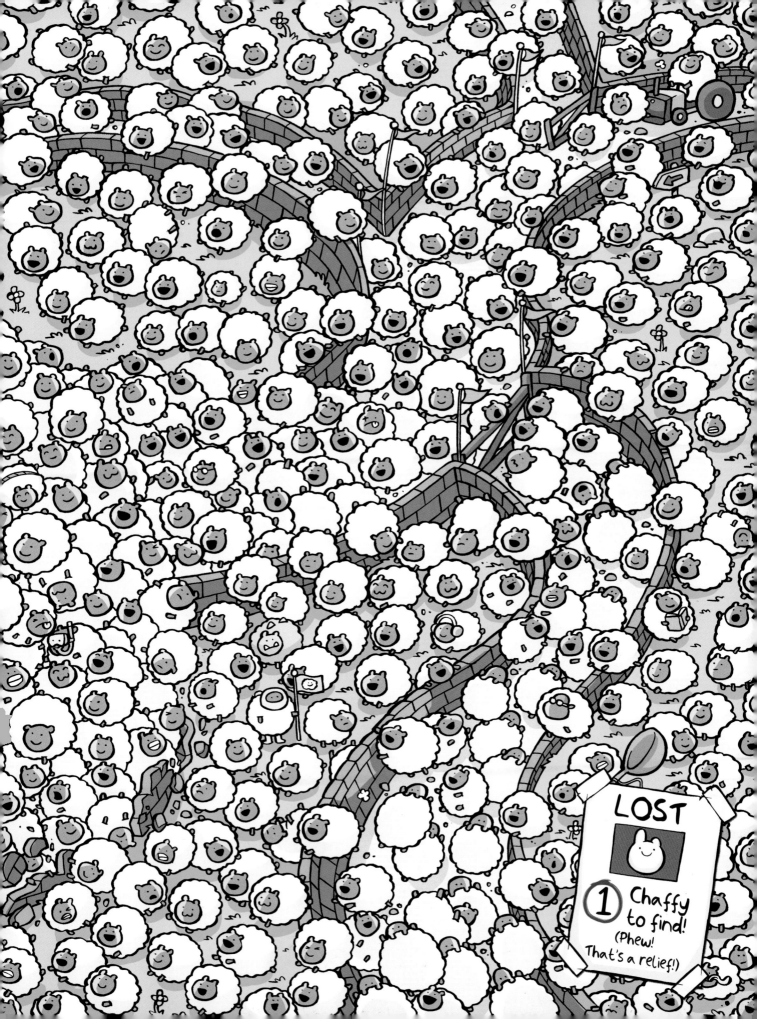

LOST

① Chaffy to find!
(Phew!
That's a relief!)

Did you find Chaffy?

What a journey we've had trying to keep these Chaffies safe and happy! But for all the dinosaurs, ghosts, kitties, pandas, octopuses, ninjas, bears, robots, sheep, and pigs we've met, there were a whole host of other ridiculous things going on along the way!

Were you eagle-eyed enough to spot THESE sights?

A panda in a plane

A panda on a unicycle

A panda driving a car

A strongman kitty

A sword-swallowing kitty

A kitty taking a dog for a walk

A ghost doing the vacuuming

A ghost on a flying bicycle

A ghost with a gas mask

A robot with a robot dog

A robot with a cat on its head

A robot with toilet paper stuck to its foot

A gnome dino
A dino having a cup of tea
A dino on a pogo stick

A pirate pig
A skiing pig
A pig taking notes

An octopus using a laptop
An octopus eating spaghetti and meatballs
A one-man band octopus

A ninja with a beard
A ninja in a tiger suit
A ninja with wings

A bear with a basket on its head
A bear having a nap
A bear on the phone

A dino sheep
A sheep with a snorkel
A surfing sheep

If you found all these, then WELL DONE! We should keep you on our team next time we're looking for any lost Chaffies!

Thank you for finding Chaffy!

(Though whether he's the Chaffy we started with, who can say for sure?)

Now this Chaffy is safe back home, let's not forget the many MANY Chaffies still lost in the world!

They're all confused, aimless, a bit stupid, and prone to ending up in ridiculous circumstances.

So we ask you politely, please be on the lookout for Chaffies. They could be anywhere! And if you ARE lucky enough to find one...

Feed him salad! (Sometimes cupcakes.)

Keep him away from lawnmowers!

Have a dance!

Give him lots and lots and LOTS of hugs.